You are WELCOME *to* GOD's FAMILY

FAITH A. OYEDEPO

You Are Welcome To God's Family

ISBN 978-2905-58-5

Published in Nigeria by:

DOMINION PUBLISHING HOUSE

Reprinted: 2013

For further information or permission, please contact:

DOMINION PUBLISHING HOUSE

Canaan Land, km 10, Idiroko Road, Ota.

P.M.B. 21688, Ikeja, Lagos, Nigeria.

Tel: 234-1-7747546-8

Web: www.davidoyedepoministries.org;
www.faithoyedepo.org

E-mail: dph@davidoyedepoministries.org

All scripture quotations are from the American King James Version of the Bible, except otherwise stated.

CONTENTS

INTRODUCTION

But as many as received him, to them gave he power to become the sons of God, even to them that believe on his name.

John 1:12

The day you accepted Jesus Christ as your Lord and Saviour, by an open confession of your faith, you made the most important decision of your life.

By this act, you are saved, born again, a child of God, and therefore have escaped the horror and penalty of sin. You become a new creature and you take on the nature of God, your heavenly Father — the nature of life. You now have eternal life!

Salvation is a spiritual rebirth. It is what qualifies you to become a member of the family of God.

Please be aware that only those who are saved and born again, can become members of this global winning family.

Now that you are born again, I specially welcome you to this exemplary family. However, you need a good understanding of your new status in this new family, if you must make the most of it.

This explains why the Bible clearly declares:

> ***Good understanding giveth favour: but the way of transgressors is hard.***
>
> Proverbs 13:15

When you have a good understanding of

your rights, privileges, responsibilities and what obtains in this family, you will be eternally taken from the miry clay and set upon the rock to rule and reign on the earth. I tell you, your status will surely change for the better!

This book is written specifically to give you the understanding you require, now that you are born again and have become a member of this winning family. It will enlighten you on what the Christian race has to offer you.

Assuredly, you will become a living proof and a wonder to your world, as you put to work the light you contact from this book.

Welcome on board the winning life!

1 THE FAMILY OF GOD

For all have sinned, and come short of the glory of God;

Romans 3:23

There is a special family on earth today, which enjoys tremendous peace, despite the chaos that is looming in the world. This family has no fear for lack or want, and this same family represents another kingdom on earth (Colossians 1:13).

The head of this glorious family is the Almighty God Himself, the Source and Creator of every good thing in life (James 1:17).

The membership of this family is for as many as are redeemed by the precious Blood of Jesus Christ, by accepting his substitutionary death on the cross, his burial, resurrection and ascension.

One time in scriptures, Jesus told a parable concerning the kingdom of heaven, likening it to a certain king who made a marriage for his son and bade many to the feast (Matthew 22:1-14).

However, when the king who invited the guests came in to see them, he saw a man who had no wedding garment on. He was ordered to be bound hand and foot and taken away. May your destiny not be bound!

That spiritual wedding garment that you require to be accepted in the kingdom, I believe is salvation!

I want you to realize that only those who are saved, born again and have become Christians can become members of this great winning family of God. "What is salvation?," you may ask.

What Salvation Is

Salvation means deliverance from the legal punishment for a committed crime/sin, which is punishable under the law of God. The offender does not have the power to deliver himself; he needs another man who is just to stand in for him.

Mankind inherited the nature of sin from Adam, and no man is free from the punishment of sin, which is death. But salvation from the horror of sin is through Jesus Christ only. Jesus' main mission on earth is to save man from sin and its consequences.

> ***For the wages of sin is death; but the gift of God is eternal life through Jesus Christ our Lord.***
>
> Romans 6:23

Please be aware that the physical death is not the end of a man, but a passage to either eternal life in glory or eternal destruction in hell. But God did not intend man to be destroyed in hell, which is why He made provision for the way out. John 3:16 says:

> ***For God so loved the world, that he gave his only begotten Son, that whosoever***

believeth in him should not perish, but have everlasting life.

As Adam's sin was inherited, so also we inherit eternal life through Jesus Christ. Anyone that acknowledges this provision will not be destroyed, but whosoever rejects this one way, will be condemned.

At salvation, the glory that was lost is restored and we regain back our fellowship with God who is our father. "But how can I be saved?," you may ask.

How To Be Saved

Salvation is not obtainable by just keeping the laws of God, but by believing in the death, resurrection and ascension of Jesus Christ, as the only way to God. The Bible says:

For with the heart man believeth

unto righteousness; and with the mouth confession is made unto salvation.

Romans 10:10

To be born again and become a member of God's family, you must believe God's Word in your heart and confess it with your mouth as stated in the above scripture. When you do this in sincerity, you will be accepted before God, just as if you never sinned. This is very important.

The question I would like to ask you right now is: Are you saved? If you are, great; you are already a member of God's family. In case you are not, or you are not sure, you can be saved right now by praying this simple prayer right now, with faith in your heart.

Salvation Prayer

Oh God, I come to You today in the name of Jesus Christ. Be merciful to me, a sinner. Forgive me my sins. I accept Jesus Christ as my Lord and Saviour today. I receive the gift of eternal life. Thank You father, for now I know that I am born again; I am a child of God. In Jesus' name I pray. Amen.

Salvation is not a secret thing, but a public affair. Your family membership is guaranteed, **only** when you give your life to Jesus Christ, by accepting Him as your personal Lord and Saviour!

When you accept Jesus Christ as Lord and Saviour, you are the one to benefit. "What do I stand to gain by so doing?," you may ask. Let's briefly mention some of them here.

BENEFITS OF SALVATION

> ***Saying with a loud voice, Worthy is the Lamb that was slain to receive power, and riches, and wisdom, and strength, and honor, and glory, and blessing.***
>
> Revelation 5:12

Life in Jesus Christ is full of gains. All that the devil had stolen is restored. Scripturally, these benefits are yours when you give your life to Jesus Christ, and you can begin to enjoy them.

- **Eternal/Everlasting Life**

> ***He that believeth on the Son hath everlasting life: and he that believeth not***

the Son shall not see life; but the wrath of God abideth on him.

John 3:36

· Peace With God

Therefore being justified by faith, we have peace with God through our Lord Jesus Christ:

Romans 5:1

· Joy

Thou hast made known to me the ways of life; thou shalt make me full of joy with thy countenance.

Acts 2:28

· Blessings

That the blessing of Abraham might come on the Gentiles through Jesus Christ; that we might receive the promise of the Spirit through faith.

Galatians 3:14

· Good Health

Beloved, I wish above all things that thou mayest prosper and be in health, even as thy soul prospereth.

3 John 1:2

· Abundance

And ye shall eat in plenty, and be satisfied, and praise the name of the LORD your God, that hath dealt wondrously with you: and my people shall never be ashamed.

Joel 2:26

· Prosperity

If they obey and serve him, they shall

spend their days in prosperity, and their years in pleasures.

Job 36:11

These benefits and many more are yours.

2 GROW SPIRITUALLY

As newborn babes, desire the sincere milk of the word, that ye may grow thereby:

1 Peter 2:2

Salvation is a birth into a growing life. When you accept Jesus Christ as your personal Lord and Saviour, you are born into the family of God. Thereafter, you are expected to keep growing spiritually.

So, it is not enough to be born again and belong to the family of God, you must grow spiritually. Growth means continuous positive changes!

When a child is born, he does not remain at the baby stage for ever. Every child is expected to keep growing, and pass from the stage of childhood to adulthood. This explains why the Bible says:

> ***When I was a child, I spake as a child, I understood as a child, I thought as a child: but when I became a man, I put away childish things.***
>
> I Corinthians 13:11

As a mother, I am aware that no parent takes pride in a child that does not grow. The desire and joy of every parent is to see their children grow.

I have watched with amazement, and seen all our biological children grow from babyhood to adulthood! They are still growing! This gives me a great pleasure and a sense of gratitude to God.

I want you to know that as it is in the natural, so it is in the spiritual. If growth is required in the natural, it is even required more in the spiritual.

At every stage of development, however, every child requires quality food for healthy growth.

In the same vein, when you are born again and become a member of God's family, you require quality spiritual food so you can grow spiritually. This is what the scripture in I Peter 2:2 explains.

"What is this spiritual food?," you may ask. It is the Word of God! God's Word, the Bible, is the food of the spirit that helps you grow after salvation.

A new born baby starts with milk and water; later he graduates to solid foods and with time he starts to crack bones. The milk, the meat and the bone of spiritual development that you need are found in the Word of God, the Bible.

For you to grow spiritually, you cannot do without the Word of God, the Bible! Your Christian growth and maturity is absolutely dependent on your intake and practice of it!

I want you to know that the Word of God, the Bible, is a personal message to you from God Almighty Himself! God's Word is alive (John 6:63) and through it, God reveals Himself to you.

God is so mindful of you that He sends

you His Word for your day-to-day living.

Please be aware that the Bible is not just a set of rules! No! Rather, it is a practical reference Book, meant to enable you live a successful Christian life.

Study it, read it, commit it to heart, meditate upon it and act on it accordingly! Don't just religiously give it a place of honour on your book shelf! It is for living!

But, why do I have to study the Bible and give it such a prominent place in my life, especially considering my daily busy schedule?

Consider the following carefully:

- **Your primary weapon of warfare**

Life is a battlefield (I Timothy 6:12)! But the good news is that you are more than a conqueror (Romans 8:37), destined to win all battles of life!

However, for this to become a reality in your life, you need to be adequately equipped. You have to put on the whole armour of God (Ephesians 6:11)

The Bible says:

> ***For the word of God is quick, and powerful, and sharper than any two edged sword, piercing even to the dividing asunder of soul and spirit, and of the joints and marrow, and is a discerner of the thoughts and intents of the heart.***
>
> Hebrews 4:12

The Word of God is our primary weapon of warfare in the battles of life.

Jesus overcame the temptations of the devil, by engaging the written Word. Three times He told the devil, ***"It is written"*** and the devil fled from Him (Luke 4: 4, 8, 12).

· It delivers your inheritance

Your inheritance in Christ, (which includes all things that make for life and godliness) are delivered unto you through your knowledge of the Word of God.

> ***According as his divine power hath given unto us all things that pertain unto life and godliness, through the knowledge of him that hath called us to glory and virtue:***
>
> 2Peter 1:3

The importance of this cannot be over-emphasized!

· It cleanses

The Word of God, the Bible, has a

cleansing power; it has the ability to wash and re-programme all that your sinful nature has written on your mind.

> ***That he might sanctify and cleanse it with the washing of water by the word,***
>
> Ephesians 5:26

· It establishes your freedom

The Word of God, the Bible is the only source of true liberty and freedom. It is an open door to your freedom in every area of life.

> ***And ye shall know the truth, and the truth shall make you free.***
>
> John 8:32

If the Bible, the Word of God is this important, how can you study it so you can benefit maximally from it? Let us briefly examine this here!

- **Make a decision**

  First, you need to make a quality decision, followed by a serious determination to study the Bible. When these are in place, it becomes easy to follow through in your actual study.

- **Allocate a period of study to it**

  It is important that you allocate a period of time for the study of the Bible. This could be either a particular time of the day, a specific length of time, in a particular place or a combination. Personally, I prefer the early hours of the day, in the morning.

It is important for you to be consistent. But in case you miss out on it once in awhile, never give room to self-condemnation. Get back on track!

- **Get a personal Bible**

Get your own personal Bible that you can use for study; do not cultivate the habit of borrowing someone's Bible for use.

There are different translations of the Bible, but for a start, I would really recommend the King James Version. This is what I use most of the time, even up till now. You may also add the Amplified Bible to it.

As you study the Bible, you can underline scriptures that have special meaning to you. This will make the Word of God become more real and personal.

You can even write and make notes right inside your Bible. Personally, I do this a lot and I can assure you that it really works.

- **Start right!**

For a start, begin your study of the Bible from the New Testament. This is not to suggest that you should not read other sections of the Bible, rather, it is to make you spend more time in studying the New Testament.

Of course, for a balanced Christian life, you need to study the whole Bible.

However, for new believers, I usually recommend starting from the books of Matthew, Mark, Luke, etc, to Revelations.

- **Read and think!**

As you read the Bible, spend time and think deeply about what you read. Meditate on the Word. Ponder and reflect continuously on what you read. To meditate is to converse within oneself.

Take in as much of the Word of God as you possibly can, each time you study it. Interestingly, there is no over-dose of it.

Read the scripture over and over again. I assure you, you will be glad you did. This helps me a great deal, personally.

- **Prayer and Word study**

Prayer and Word study go hand-in-hand. Your study of the Bible cannot be adequate without prayer and vice versa.

It is important that you pray before, during and after the study of the Bible. In prayer, ask God to open the eyes of your understanding so you can comprehend what you read in His Word.

As you read, expect God to reveal His Word to you and He will fulfill your expectations.

- **Study materials**

For effective Word study, certain support materials will be of help to you

These include Bible concordance, dictionary, computer Bible, etc. You may also get different translations of the Bible.

- **Think, speak, act and live the Word!**

  In essence, the ultimate of studying the Bible is so it can become your way of life. Acting on the Word of God is what produces results (Matthew 7:24-27).

  When your life is Word-controlled, you will always be in control! You will also keep growing spiritually.

In concluding this chapter, let me say categorically here that when your life is ruled by the Word of God, you will surely rule your world!

3 THE POWER OF PRAYER

...men ought always to pray and not to faint.

Luke 18:1(b)

Communication is the strength of every relationship. Your relationship with God, as a member of His family, has to be strengthened per day and the only way you could achieve this is by praying.

Prayer is a spiritual device by which the believer communicates with God. It is the primary communication link that you have as a Christian.

However, for your prayer to be effective and produce results, you must mind the following:

- **Pray from the heart**

  The depth of your heart from where your prayer comes is what determines whether it will produce results or not.

  The Bible says:

And ye shall seek me, and find me, when ye shall search for me with all your heart.

Jeremiah 29:13

You can only find God, when you seek Him with the whole of your heart!

- **Pray with the Word of God**

Your prayer should be in line with the Word of God, not contrary to it. This explains why the Bible says:

...if we ask anything according to his will, he heareth us:

I John5:14(b)

Only prayers according to God's will, which is His Word, will receive answers.

- **Always add thanksgiving to your prayer**

Thanksgiving should be an essential part of your prayer, for it to produce results.

Be careful for nothing; but in every thing by prayer and supplication with thanksgiving let your requests be

made known to God.

Philippians 4:6

- **Keep it simple!**

For your prayer to be effective, keep it simple. You do not need to make it become so complicated and confusing. The Bible talks about the simplicity of the gospel. II Corinthians 11:3

- **Pray in faith.**

Therefore I say unto you, What things soever ye desire, when ye pray, believe that ye receive them, and ye shall have them.

Mark 11:24

I want you to understand that when you pray, it is for your

good! This will help to make prayer exciting for you. What do you benefit by praying?

Benefits of Prayer

- **Answer to your requests!**

Call unto me, and I will answer thee, and show thee great and mighty things, which thou knowest not.

Jeremiah 33:3

- **You are equipped for warfare**

Prayer is one of our weapons of war. We war against the enemy in prayer. Because our warfare is not against flesh and blood, we fight spiritual battles and we engage spiritual weapon in prayers (2 Corinthians 10:3-5).

As you apply the Word of God in prayer, you will discover that even your struggle with sin will come to an end.

- **You are empowered**

  Obviously, prayer is the gateway to supernatural power! Conversely, to be prayerless is to be powerless (Luke 11: 1-13).

All these benefits and more become yours, when you become a praying Christian. It is time to awake unto prayer!

4 THE PLACE OF WATER BAPTISM

And there went out unto him all the land of Judea, and they of Jerusalem, and were all baptized of him in the river of Jordan, confessing their sins.

Mark 1:5

There are two types of baptism in scriptures, both of which every believer is expected to undergo. They are: The Water Baptism and The Holy Ghost Baptism.

In this chapter, we shall briefly examine The Water Baptism. The Holy Ghost

Baptism shall be treated in the next chapter.

The word 'baptize' means to totally immerse an object in another substance and then bring it out again. So, to baptize someone in water means to totally immerse the person in water and bring him out again.

The significance of Water Baptism

Carefully consider these:

- **The baptismal waters represent a burial ground.**

  When you are immersed in water during baptism, it means you are buried with Jesus Christ. This in essence means that your old self with all its sinful deeds no longer exists!

  I want you to pay particular attention to this insightful scripture:

Therefore we are buried with him by

baptism into death: that like as Christ was raised up from the dead by the glory of the Father, even so we also should walk in newness of life.

Romans 6:4

Water Baptism is one sure way to easily overcome old habits!

- **Coming out of the water represents being raised to a new life.**

  When you come out of the water after baptism, it shows that you are now raised to begin to live a new life in Christ Jesus. In effect, this means that Jesus Christ now becomes your Lord in every area of life.

  Thereafter, as the scripture says, you should begin to:

...yield yourselves unto God, as those

that are alive from the dead, and your members as instruments of righteousness unto God.

Romans 6:14

You must understand that Water Baptism symbolizes your identification with Jesus Christ in His death, burial and resurrection.

When you are baptized in water, among other things, you:

- Obey God's commandment concerning Water Baptism (Matthew 28:19).
- Openly testify to others about your born-again experience (2Corinthians 5: 17).
- Signify your readiness to walk in the newness of life (Galatians 2:20).
- Publicly declare the Lordship of Jesus

Christ over your life.

- Have fulfilled all righteousness, following the example of Jesus, because He was also baptized in water (Matthew 3: 15-17).

As I conclude this chapter, I want to ask you this all-important question: Have you been baptized in Water by immersion since you believed?

Until you do, you may not experience what it means to walk in the newness of life. Make sure you take steps immediately and get baptized in water by immersion by a Bible-believing minister, who understands the importance of Water Baptism.

Remember, it is for your good! You shall not be robbed of that which belongs to you!

5 BAPTISM OF POWER

But ye shall receive power, after that the Holy Ghost is come upon you: and ye shall be witnesses unto me both in Jerusalem, and in all Judea, and in Samaria, and unto the uttermost part of the earth.

Acts 1:8

As noted in the last chapter, there are two types of baptism in the scripture that every believer has to undergo: *The Water Baptism and The Holy Ghost Baptism*.

Water Baptism:

Is to openly proclaim that you are dead, buried and risen up with Jesus Christ. It is an open declaration of your new status as a Christian. Jesus was baptized by John at Jordan to fulfill all righteousness (Matthew 3:15). Water baptism is meant for only those that have confessed Jesus as their Lord and Saviour (Mark 1:5).

Water baptism is conducted by pastors today; but the second type of baptism, the Holy Ghost baptism, can only be performed by Jesus Christ!

Holy Ghost Baptism:

Is the infilling of the Holy Spirit with the evidence of speaking in tongues. After you are born again, God's plan and desire is that you get baptized in the Holy Spirit.

Baptism in the Holy Spirit is one of the packages of redemption. If you have given your life to Jesus, you are entitled to be filled with the Holy Ghost.

> ***Then Peter said unto them, Repent, and be baptized every one of you in the name of Jesus Christ for the remission of sins, and ye shall receive the gift of the Holy Ghost.***
>
> ***For the promise is unto you, and to your children, and to all that are afar off, even as many as the Lord our God shall call.***
>
> Acts 2:38-39

How do I receive this gift of the Holy Spirit, since it is one of the packages of redemption? Take a close look at these:

- **A genuine thirst**

To be baptized in the Holy Spirit, you must

have a genuine thirst and a strong desire in your heart. The Bible says:

> ***In the last day, that great day of the feast, Jesus stood and cried, saying, If any man thirst, let him come unto me, and drink.***
>
> John 7:37

When God sees this thirst in your heart, He will unleash upon you the gift of the Holy Spirit.

- **Ask in faith**

Ask for the baptism in the Holy Spirit in faith. When you do this, He comes to live in you. The scripture says:

> ***If ye then, being evil, know how to give good gifts unto your children: how much more shall your heavenly Father give the Holy***

Spirit to them that ask him?

Luke 11:13

As in the Book of Acts, when you are baptized in the Holy Spirit, you will speak in tongues.

Unlike the water baptism which can be conducted by any Pastor, only Jesus is the baptizer of the Holy Ghost. John the Baptist said:

> ***I indeed baptize you with water unto repentance: but he that cometh after me is mightier than I, whose shoes I am not worthy to bear: he shall baptize you with the Holy Ghost, and with fire:***
>
> ***Whose fan is in his hand, and he will throughly purge his floor, and gather his wheat into the garner; but he will burn up the chaff with unquenchable fire***

Matthew 3:11-12

So, ask Jesus, the baptizer, to baptize you with the Holy Spirit and He surely will!

- **Open your mouth and speak!**

To be baptized in the Holy Spirit, you have to do the speaking! You have to yield your mouth and tongue to the Holy Spirit.

This is why the Bible states:

> ***And they were all filled with the Holy Ghost, and began to speak with other tongues, as the Spirit gave them utterance.***
>
> Acts 2:4

The Holy Spirit will give you utterance, but you have to yield your tongue, breath and vocal cords to Him to get this done. Initially, this may seem strange to you, but continue. With time, you will grow and be able to speak fluently.

Let me say categorically here that your exploits as a Christian will be limited, if you are not baptized in the Holy Spirit. Jesus told the disciples to wait for the infilling of the Holy Spirit, before embarking on any ministerial work.

What are the benefits of being baptized in the Holy Ghost? They include but are not limited to the following:

- **Enduement with power:**

But ye shall receive power, after that the Holy Ghost is come upon you: and ye shall be witnesses unto me both in Jerusalem, and in all Judea, and in Samaria, and unto the uttermost part of the earth.

Acts 1:8

- **Help to Pray according to God's will:**

Likewise the Spirit also helpeth our infirmities: for we know not what we should pray for as we ought: but the Spirit itself maketh intercession for us with groanings which cannot be uttered.

Romans 8:26

- **He helps to build our faith**

But ye, beloved, building up yourselves on your most holy faith, praying in the Holy Ghost

Jude 1:20

- **We speak mysteries to God**

For he that speaketh in an unknown tongue speaketh not unto men, but

unto God: for no man understandeth him; howbeit in the spirit he speaketh mysteries.

1 Corinthians 14:2

- **You walk in other gifts of the Holy Spirit**

Now there are diversities of gifts, but the same Spirit.

1 Corinthians 12:4

- **You are kept pure and holy**

Whose fan is in his hand, and he will throughly purge his floor, and gather his wheat into the garner; but he will burn up the chaff with unquenchable fire.

Matthew 3:12

Consequently, if you are not baptized in the Holy Spirit, these benefits will elude you!

6 YOUR RESPONSIBILITY

For the earnest expectation of the creature waiteth for the manifestation of the sons of God.

Romans 8:19

Christianity is a life of responsibility.

You are not saved just to occupy space, neither are you endowed with the gift of the Holy Spirit, just to speak in tongues. You are expected to manifest your sonship as a member of God's family. Some of the areas where your manifestation is required include:

Fellowship with others

- You are expected to join a fellowship where you can be blessed and be a blessing. The coming together of believers is important and relevant to spiritual growth.

- The presence of God is guaranteed where His children are gathered. Matthew 18:20 says:

For where two or three are gathered together in my name, there am I in the midst of them.

- Going to church should not become a religious right; it is one of the laid down examples that the scripture gave to us. Jesus was found in the temple at the age of 12 (Luke 2:46). He also went to the synagogue where He read from the scriptures and read what was written concerning Him (Luke 4:16-21).

* Also, you are edified through the ministerial gifts of others. You hear seasoned Word from the pulpit, edifying songs/psalms, prayers, prophecies, etc. You, also, will be developed in exercising the use of your spiritual gift.

* The reason why many are not 'in touch' with God is because they are not 'in church'.

Be a shining light.

The Bible calls believers the light of the

earth. Matthew 5:14 says:

> ***Ye are the light of the world. A city that is set on a hill cannot be hid.***

As light, you are to show others the way and lead them to Christ. Let your life be a living testimony that will draw unbelievers to Christ. Refuse to become a stumbling block in the lives of others! You can always turn to the Holy Spirit, to lead you in all things.

Get involved in kingdom service

One of your responsibilities as a member of God's family is service. Locate a place where you can serve in the Body of Christ!

> ***And ye shall serve the Lord your God, and he shall bless thy bread, and thy water; and I will take sickness away***

from the midst of thee.

Exodus 23:25

Refuse to just occupy space, without supplying something to the overall growth of the kingdom of God to which you now belong. This explains why the scriptures declare:

From whom the whole body fitly joined together and compacted by that which every joint supplieth, according to the effectual working in the measure of every part, maketh increase of the body unto the edifying of itself in love.

Ephesians 4:16

As a joint in the Body of Christ, there is something that you are meant to supply, which will make for the overall growth and increase of the body.

Be a witness

Soul-winning is the heartbeat of God, especially this end-time! Jesus, while He was on earth, said:

> ***Therefore said he unto them, The harvest truly is great, but the labourers are few: pray ye therefore the Lord of the harvest, that he would send forth laborers into his harvest.***
>
> Luke 10:2

You are one of the end-time soldiers that have been enlisted to preach to as many as are yet to be saved.

Soul-winning enhances both your wisdom level (Proverbs 11:30), as well as your shining in the kingdom of heaven. Daniel 12:3 *says:*

> ***And they that be wise shall shine as the***

brightness of the firmament; and they that turn many to righteousness as the stars forever and ever.

Manifest the fruits of the Spirit

As a member of God's family, you are expected to manifest the fruits of the Spirit. This is the only evidence that you truly belong to God.

The ability to manifest these fruits is already deposited into you by the Holy Spirit. Galatians 5:22-23 says:

But the fruit of the Spirit is love, joy, peace, longsuffering, gentleness, goodness, faith, Meekness, temperance: against such there is no law.

As you put the light you have contacted in this book to work, you become a fruitful member of the ever-winning global family of God.

In your light, may others see light!

The Author

Faith Abiola Oyedepo has through the leading of the Holy Spirit, brought hope, joy, peace and life into many families and homes in her generation.

For many years that she received the ministry for families and homes, she has in no little measure dedicated her entire life to showing people the perfect will of God concerning their family relationships and homes. Her regular and scintillating weekly newspaper and internet columns - Family Matters, Family Success and Family Life, among others - have helped in no small way in achieving this goal.

Also, she is reaching out to the less privileged, the needy and those in the valley of decision, through her Faith Abiola Oyedepo Foundation (FAOF).

She has a divine mandate to make her shoulders available and enrich the lives of singles and unmarried persons in a unique way.

Pastor Faith has written over 20 anointed and impactful books that have transformed many lives and given them a change of story, including her best-selling title: *Rescued From Destruction*.

An anointed preacher of the Gospel, Pastor Faith has been doggedly supportive of her husband [Dr. David O. Oyedepo, the Visionary/President Of Living Faith Church Worldwide Inc.] in the work of the ministry.

They are the parents of four grown children – David Jnr., Isaac, Love and Joys.

Books By The Author

- Building A Successful Family
- Making Marriage Work
- Success In Marriage
  (Co-authored with Dr. David Oyedepo)
- Marriage Covenant
- Raising Godly Children
- Rescued From Destruction
- Single With A Difference
- The Effective Minister's Wife
- The Spirit Of Faith
- A Living Witness (Expanded version)
- Nurturing The Incorruptible Seed (Expanded version)
- Service: The Master Key (Expanded version)
- The Dignity Of The Believer (Expanded version)
- Growing In Grace
- The Power Of The Communion Table
- Healing, Health And Wholeness
- Overcoming Anxiety
- Salvation: The Way Of Escape
- The Healing Scriptures
- The Healing Ministry Of Jesus Christ
- You Are Welcome To God's Family
- Understanding Motherhood

INSIDE VIEW OF Faith Tabernacle

OUTSIDE VIEW OF FAITH TABERNACLE

CHURCH MASS TRANSIT— Over 250 buses commuting the worshippers to Church from all nook and crannies of Lagos & environs

Dr. David Oyedepo is the founding president of the Living Faith Church Worldwide Inc. And senior pastor of the Faith Tabernacle, a 50,000 capacity sanctuary located in Canaan Land, Ota, a suburb of Lagos Nigeria.

The construction of this gigantic architectural masterpiece was completed within twelve months and dedicated on September 18, 1999. Built totally debt free and without any foreign inputs! To God alone be all the glory.

Today, Faith Tabernacle stands as the home of signs and wonders for men and women all over the world who keep coming in droves to worship the King of kings and Lord of lords, Jesus Christ the Son of the Living God.

Visit our website for more information: www.davidoyedepoministries.org

Aerial View Of Covenant University

College of Business & Social Sciences

More Facilities@ Covenant University

College of Science & Technology

University Library (Centre For Learning Resources)

4,000 Seat Students Chapel

More Facilities@ Covenant University

Post Graduate Building

Senior Staff Residential Quarters

Covenant University 100 Room Ultra Modern Guest House

Students Hall Of Residence

More Facilities@ Landmark University

University Chapel

College Building

Cafetaria

More Facilities@Landmark University

One of the Student's Halls Of Residence

Professors Village

Staff Quarters